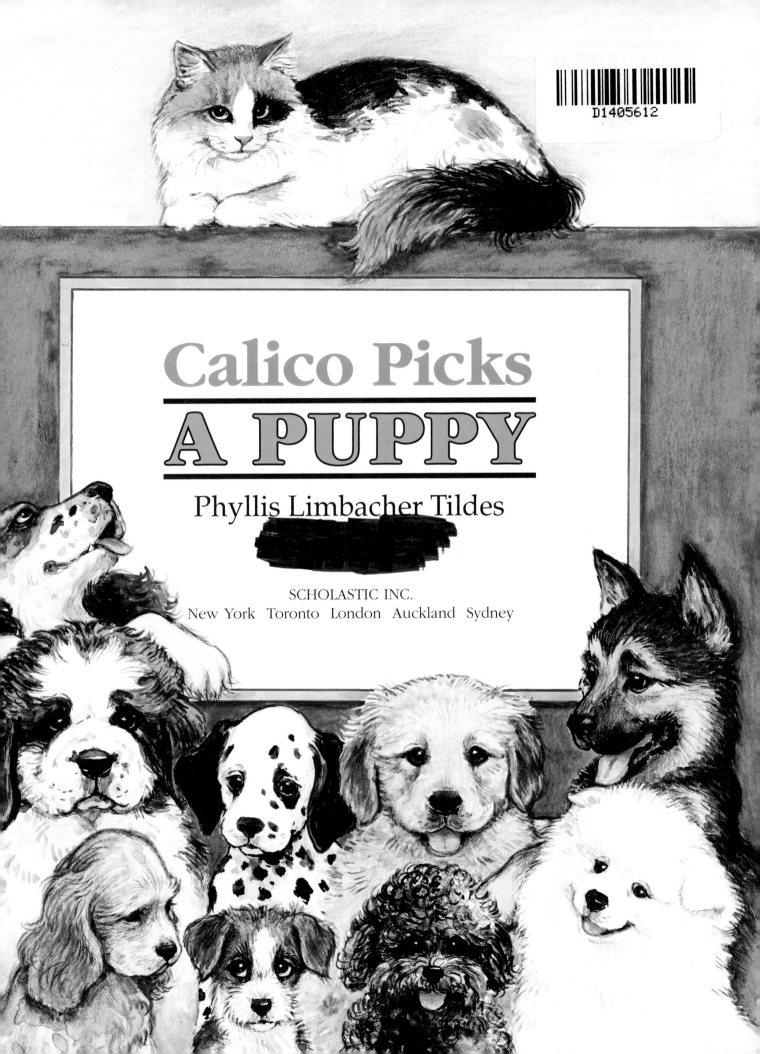

Calico Picks
A PUPPY

Phyllis Limbacher Tildes

SCHOLASTIC INC.
New York   Toronto   London   Auckland   Sydney

For Bill and Jeff, with love

With special thanks to my editor,
Elena Dworkin Wright,
for her creative contributions

ISBN 0-590-30744-4

Text and illustrations copyright © 1996 by Phyllis Limbacher Tildes. All rights reserved. Published by Scholastic Inc., 555 Broadway, New York, NY 10012, by arrangement with Charlesbridge Publishing.

12 11 10 9 8 7 6 5 4 3 2   7 8 9/9 0 1 2/0

Printed in the U.S.A.   14

First Scholastic printing, February 1997

Hello,
my name is Calico,
and I'm looking for
the *purr*fect pet puppy.

Puppies come in so
many colors and shapes.
Let me show you
some of my favorites.

Poodles are performers.

Romping in the park or performing tricks, these pups are the center of attention.

Poodles are so smart they can learn to do tricks like dancing in circles on their hind legs. Their soft, curly coat does not shed. It can be clipped into many fancy shapes and styles.

Retrievers like to carry things.

These two lively pups will be "dog tired" after fetching all day. They carry things gently in their soft mouths.

Golden Retrievers are big, strong, and eager to please. **Labrador Retrievers** are so reliable that they are trained as guide dogs for the blind.

Spaniels spring and splash.

 Any warm puppy would love a cool pool in the "dog days" of summer, but spaniels love playing in water any time of the year.

This **American Cocker Spaniel**, black-and-white **English Cocker Spaniel**, and brown-and-white **Springer Spaniel** have long, wavy coats that will drip-dry in the sun.

Sheepdogs and Shepherds enjoy a job.

What could be more fun than kitten sittin'?
These pups are kind and affectionate and
don't mind an *itty, bitty, kitty bite.*

Old English Sheepdogs
are large and shaggy.
Like sheep, their woolly
fur can be sheared
and made into cozy
sweaters. Their
unusual bark
sounds like a deep
ringing bell.

German Shepherds
are big, strong, and
easily trained for many
tasks. They have great
intelligence and excellent
hearing. These dogs
can hear a whistle
a mile away.

Hounds are sensational sniffers.

 Hounds' noses know scents up to one million times better than human noses do!

Dachshunds may be shaped like hot dogs, but their short legs cover lots of ground with enthusiasm.
Beagles are curious hounds that love to roam. They can sniff their way home if they ever get lost.
Basset Hounds have droopy eyes and the longest ears of any dog. They follow trails with their big, wet noses to the ground. Wetness helps the nose pad pick up scent particles in the air. No two dogs' nose pads are ever the same. Each nose print is unique, like a human fingerprint.

Collies can count sheep

... whether awake or asleep.

Collies are natural herders of geese, sheep, or even kittens and use any chance to demonstrate their abilities. Even when these pups are sleeping, their paws twitch as if they are dreaming about herding sheep.

Rough-Coated Collies, like Lassie, are loyal and devoted to people. **Border Collies** act as if they are trying to hypnotize sheep with their eyes.

Setter pups stir things up.

Get ready, get set, go! Setters are good-natured pets that need lots of exercise. They will wave their tails enthusiastically while following the scent of an animal. Adult setters hold still or "set" when they get close to a bird. That's why they are called setters.

Irish Setters have silky, red coats and independent spirits.
Black-and-brown **Gordon Setters** and spotted **English Setters** can run all day through fields and streams.

Let's size up this situation!

No bones about it,
this little pup has gumption.

Chihuahua pups grow up to be the tiniest dogs of all — small enough to fit in your pocket. They are so feisty and fearless, they act as if they don't know they are small. They are loyal companions and will act like a watchdog, barking at intruders of any size.

Great Dane pups are as gentle as they are big . . . in other words, real "pussycats." When they grow up to be 135 pounds, they have a bark big enough to scare people away. But neither a Chihuahua nor a Great Dane makes a good guard dog. One is feisty but too little; the other is big but too kind.

Terriers are terrific diggers.

 Terriers are rugged, spunky little puppies. Like cats, they love to chase rodents. When a terrier finds a burrow, it may bark and dig frantically. Even though some terriers are small, they are remarkably courageous.

Black **Scottish Terriers**, brown-and-white **Jack Russells**, and other small terriers will go right down a hole. **Airedales** are too big, but enjoy digging and barking. Chasing a chipmunk is a great game, and this chipmunk is winning.

Snow dogs wish for winter.

At home in the coldest weather, these pups love to frolic in snow. Their thick fur keeps them dry and warm.

Chow Chow pups might be mistaken for bouncy teddy bears. They are rust, black, tan, gray, or white and are the only breed of dog with a blue-black tongue.

Siberian Huskies are still used to pull sleds in the snowy north. Huskies may howl like a wolf instead of barking, but they are usually very quiet.

Samoyeds are also very strong sled dogs. Their white fur is so thick that they almost look like furry snowmen.

Lap dogs are cuddly.

 Any size lap will do for these little puppies!

Pugs are clever and comical. They have smooth, velvety fur and curlicue tails. Instead of barking, they grunt, snort, and snuffle.

Lhasa Apso pups will look like silky mops when they grow up. This dog is called the "frontwards backwards" dog because its fur hangs down to the floor and you can't tell whether it is coming or going.

Bichon Frise pups are curly, white balls of fluff.
This toy-sized dog is very affectionate and entertaining.

Mountain dogs are gentle giants.

Whether on a mountain or a mole hill, these large pups like to be outdoors.

Great Pyrenees may be the most powerful dog of all. They are built for life on the rugged mountains between Spain and France.

Saint Bernards are brave dogs that have saved many lives in the storms and avalanches of the Swiss Alps.

Bernese Mountain Dogs are strong enough to pull children in a cart. They are gentle and calm companions.

Wrinkles and spots are special.

Some say that beauty is skin deep.
Others say that beauty is in the eye of the beholder.
Either way, these puppies are perfect.

Shar Pei pups look like they
are wearing oversized coats.
As they grow, their skin
will fit better but will
always have extra folds.

Dalmatians may be a bit "dotty," but they are not born spotty. This puppy began life all white. As she gets older, she develops a pattern of personal punctuation marks.

What about
mixed-breed puppies?

A mix of two (or more) breeds may result in a puppy
with the best features of both parents. Mixed-breed
dogs come in many shapes, colors, and sizes.
They can be wonderful pets and playmates.
Could this be "puppy love"?

I think I've found my *purr*fect match!
Just like me he has a patch.
There is no need to tame him,
But you can help me name him.